KEVIN DAVIES

EDGE

Parts of this book appeared in *The Capilano Review* (ed. Catriona Strang), *The Delineator* (ed. Larry Fagin), and *Best American Experimental Writing 2016* (Wesleyan University Press, eds. Charles Bernstein and Tracie Morris). Earlier versions were read at Johns Hopkins University (Chris Nealon) and the Segue Reading Series (Corina Copp and Charity Coleman). The author also acknowledges the support of the Canada Council and the Fund for Poetry. And many thanks to Thomas Evans, Rod Smith, and Deirdre Kovac for their editorial and design work.

ALSO BY THE AUTHOR
The Golden Age of Paraphernalia (Edge Books, 2008)
Comp., trans. Xandaire Sélène (Le Quartanier, 2006)
Lateral Argument (Barretta Books, 2003)
Comp. (Edge Books, 2000)
Pause Button (Tsunami Editions, 1992)

ISBN: 978-1-890311-49-0

Edge Books are published by Rod Smith, editor of *Aerial* magazine, and distributed by Small Press Distribution, Berkeley, CA; 1-800-869-7553; www.spdbooks.org.

Edge Books
P.O. Box 25642, Georgetown Station
Washington, D.C. 20027

aerialedge@gmail.com   www.aerialedge.com

They crawl on me that sometimes do me bite who
live behind boards in what's seen as blindness and unite
behind compulsion to avoid annihilation sew themselves
       in new alignments through
               perplexing demonstration. Later a game
possibly descended from baseball played over curved distances
       with theory-neutral metal discs and platforms.

.

So
       who owns this horse called Red?
                     Is it me? *Am I Red?*

.

Don't wait in stairwell for answer. *Get
back to work.* Drive off in sudden car. *Roam Earth.*
Apollo wants you to sweep up thoroughly once a week
       and just generally keep shit off the floor.
If Jehovah's Witnesses come by, he wants you to be polite but silent.
Three feet beneath the surface of the garden
       lurk the remains of an ancient seems-like root cellar.
He wants you to keep that sealed up no matter what.
Got it? OK, back to the hell you were doing.
               Chopping or whatever.

.

Always a second half to the apartment forgotten
A running-to-seed luxury suite with vortex baths and plush if dusty couches and
we always just about to do the laundry far too late to make a difference.
The source of embarrassment found to be a large freestanding testicle pulsing
       radioactively at rear of cabinet removed with tongs and set free in the
       incinerator out back.

.

The lease hieroglyphic won't stand up to courtroom
                    violence when it comes to that.
We could set our watches by it if we still had watches instead of
          wristless timepieces embedded as journalists here and there and
          computer adjusted via satellite. Dang
the terms of our contracts, dang them.
The codicils of our agreements–fie.
These upended tureens of red powder do not augur restful contemplation.
I scry with an operated-on, cataract-free right eye
          a Murphy-bed catastrophe built into the very wall
          of this-here what-do-you-call-it-all
                    sounds of paper tearing slowly.

                    •

Crenellation appears where crenellation had not
          previously been thought of or desired
lending a Pringle-ish contour to the underside of reality.
Two literary scholars from outer space
          able to speak and be understood because
                    of a drug we all took
                              which is wearing off.

                    •

Dreams themselves are persons having fits in changing rooms.
I've brought the new opera CD to acknowledge all your hard work roasting the swan
and somehow find myself underneath the car poking
          randomly with a wrench for signs of pain.

                    •

I'd like to work anthropologically with civil engineers
          for a decade or so of thick description.
Do you have butter to go with this straw?
          The billions of times I've asked that question
                    across all the exfoliating multiverses never
                              the same, always some flower
                                        arrangement altered or cub

scout with three noses
. . . just as the last trailers are expelled from the park
and glue traps set against return of tenants . . .

•

There's evidence we must have thought
            highly of ourselves in later epochs
I can't drink from anything called appallingly a snifter.
Sobriety shows no it within.
Drunkenness inflates a membrane
            on which a face is painted.
That's your choice right there.

•

Semiautonomous malware within the conglomerate obliterated
            some components beyond even memory and others
            it demoted from honored cubes to mere squares.

•

Friendly mockery is always real mockery, we thought you knew.
It's at the stitching we're most likely to burst
            or simply fall apart into individual nerves
                        deprived of their network squirt impulse into void.

•

I counted aloud all the numbers between 2.4 and 19.3B7. It took forever

•

            And maybe that's OK back in Roman Britain but not here.
Here we are cooking dinner later in a futurist yurt,
birds of yore transformed to land scramblers
            keen to chair their own district meetings,
traces of light copyedit in the fossil record.

•

We need a new electronic journal that refuses words,
        sounds, images, and we need it now
to hover somewhere behind us and yet deeply
        beneath Io's jagged surface in a lockbox,
all user data harvested for analysis, sulfur-dioxide frost.
And we need it to be written off by cops as one of their own drunken pranks.

•

I've been examining your sputum under the microscope
        and have found imhomogeneities that will likely doom us all
        and bring an end to this wretched but lovely simulation.
In place of hair a sort of old-age down sprouts up uncombable,
Theban in persistence, Corsican in martial ardor,
Venezuelan in desire to stone the vice president.

•

The thing about things in themselves is they're snobs as I see it
The manner by which a cultural product rises from mulch
equivalent to any number of star systems
        berating the cook for inept consommé,
the ibid factor, limpets on underside
        adhere to strict policy of spore erosion.

•

Hiccups of gray parrots syncopate the exit interview.
Everything arranged in nonparallel lists. Surnames decay.
Even cats of this world chase ghost doubles down holes.

•

There ought to be a term for the leftover
        bit of time after the strategy meeting
and before full reengagement with line charts

depicting aspect of social media squirrels interacting with content.
We should each have thimble-sized cakes, each with a tiny candle,
and there should be some sort of coded vibraphone narration
leading us around each other in figure eights.

·

All the old tire-swing swimming holes now shown
through the symbols of formal logic to have been indoor
all along.
Of course I admire Putin's assault on creative writing programs
but I feel self-conscious speaking English in this alley.

·

The only mammal that can simultaneously descend
the tree face first and refuse to do so.

·

It's not denial, it's repression, it's like a ligament,
try walking around without it. It
isn't *for* you to say. It isn't *for* you
in any important way.

·

Have to work right through dinner translating
the description of a salmon dish marred by
berries of some sort, cran- or blue-, not in the
original recipe and possibly added a week ago by me
eating now this microwaved thing with French
text before me though I don't know a word except
arrêt, alouette, and *je te plumerai la tête*.

·

All those fancy people who scored higher on tests
are seated at a different table with different food.
The replicative protocols must be met with violence.

•

Earth's relegation to planetoid has fucked with reception and everyone's balance.
A guy, Bob, turns up to hang briefly with my parent.
Earth's new name is Hamish.

•

The valley on the other side pictures a bear
        abutting the historical rise of heavy industry.
A proper wayfarer will understand the intermediateness
        of actually everything but especially this.

•

Don't stomp the Jains sleeping on the downslope.
Reassemble yourself from parts of adverbs, qualifiers of actions
        lacking for a moment the waddling monotremic subject.
This is heaven. You've arrived and must burn it down.

•

We worry about delivery drones. Most of these workers
        are settling into their late styles–genre blur,
        abrupt transition, choral disputation.

•

A cat won't eat oatmeal unless you put fish in it.
You can now learn this from your phone.
We had only trial and error. Oh there were libraries
        but they were weak on feline nutrition,
surprisingly strong on sorcery and witchcraft
so that I sprang forth a full-fledged 8-year-old scholiast of nature's
        dark powers, so that if perhaps I could not entice
        the cat to eat oatmeal, I could at least transform the beast
        into a Pentecostal.

•

As for those who take a dim view of you,
        best to retreat at a measured pace from the intersection
        and pretend to lie low while plotting ambush.
This entire civilization is built on revenge.
An enemy is another self.

        •

Kids must be great for the résumé. One of them, too slow,
        the smallest, must enter the dormitory and become a demon.

        •

A small army of bugs has ventured via left ear to precipice of brain.
They behold there the astounding fat content with awe.
With this we can grow a larger and more livid queen.
Which is how we need to consider the coming singularity.

        •

Watch now: The constable is in for a big surprise, and he's armed.

        •

Far away, where the geoduck farmers sport and play,
the future is being decided by ghost Germans.
Even idiots had gallerists those days. Especially!
How else to calculate the worth of our loads?

        •

Now listen here. I'm the editor. I'm the editor.
        I just can't seem to find my shirt.

        •

I'm employed to make tiny revisions to product warnings.
We are sometimes required to remove banned letters R and M
        from the reading experience of the doomed.

·

They found burnt land, and they found things would grow in it.
They took mental notes.
They had sentences but no sense of individual words.
They presumably looked sort of like us.
Grooming was more complex because underfunded.
They had no writing and thus no semicolons but
                    strangely did have hyphens.

·

No more socks, no more underwear–they've been used up.
No more novels about banking–they exhaust the soul with incident.
If this is an enterprisewide initiative, everyone who earlier
          must have got stoned must now unfurl the banner.

·

These tweezers were on special. They almost work.
Why did the living partner think it apt to narrate the late pieces?
If there's one thing Jake hates it's more than one hippie.

·

You have to clear out everything and douse it.
Otherwise you will be a vector. Do you want that?
To say you're welcome is to exaggerate.
          Now you know. You're welcome.

·

          Let us continue up this path awhile
as though I'm a Browning narrator and you're the croupier
                    of my daughter's dealer.

·

The salt levels of our various tolerances are how we're sorted.
It's nothing personal. The gadget-level loop
        of instructional narration is a dominant art.

                        •

Tiny scalp registrations. Burglar acting nonchalant.
The toddler addresses the bottle of sparkling wine
        as though an unbalanced colleague.

                        •

Some say "they worked like devils" but I always imagined
devils as very lazy, standing around drinking grape pop
and ridiculing the A students, which is why I wanted
to be one, a devil.

                        •

The new front-door password is complicated and requires
        one to soak torso in grease before approach.
                This tends to weed out dilettantes.

                        •

Into the plasma of the undifferentiated
        rode the nine kabillion, sideways.
Earlier either I or a cousin of yours who stands for me
had been out all night with a notorious woman, stealing cattle.

                        •

The movie in synthetic Scots is just an hour and a half
        of Mary Poppins trying and failing to take a bath
        in an old tin tub previously used for scalding foxes.

                        •

The it awakens each morning, if it does, to a note
       of greeting and appreciation for great Baal,
            usurper of the spinning brunch entrée that is this.
I drop from the ceiling onto the shoulders of my older self
       who accuses me of being the biological father of its youngest child.

      •

I sensed the group of which I formed a part could turn.
Or rather I myself was group of parts attached
       nonrandomly to tails and flanks of mutating conveyances,
            the weight of one thing bending
      attention of another.
So how do I go about having myself collected as object?
Must I prove provenance, if prove is what one
      does with that? Is it OK to use electrical tape
      to obscure the gearbox? When my peripheral members
      permanently lose consciousness, can a bit of the lather be
      saved in a stoppered tube for later evaluation?
      What say if any does one, I mean me, do I have
      in terms of storage companies?

      •

She should have moved the house rather than kill the tree.

      •

      I hear the horn of the mayor
as an antic popular cartoon show will live on as the age's
      greatest art, fully cargo-culted in dank
        gullies of exo-moons.
         A third-person I—a Dog—a bed
      that can be driven like a car—head
     covered in goop unwashable after the water runs out
which is what precipitated violence to lamp—

      •

Fellow toilers not lately seen
        when asked where they'd been answered "go there"
           and "across the street."

      •

All those extras worked for sandwiches *if lucky*.
Yes, it's a two-headed coin—*but whose head?*
                —the long stare
        out the window, across scrap-metal remains,
        into the stricken face of a Presbyterian sommelier.

      •

I've missed most of the sale. The clothes a dollar
             that fall off the rack.
Everyone too hungry to move.
           I've come here to bet on professional bingo.
        I have a system. It calls to me.

      •

We were finishing each other's sentence fragments,
        grunts, gestures, tics, and dead silent
           immobility by the time soldiers were proposed as being
           outside the hut and bent on entry.

      •

So don't talk to me about claustrophobia.

seems to argue that true names begin in
imitation of motion or stasis can certainly
not be deemed arbitrary I mean what would
that perforce make us

Initiated cognition sequence already a mistake jam-
packed intergalactic communication package terrible failure
of taste to find fine hose like this in a corner
store of the old school beyond the adjudication of chance former planet
Pluto in its new job terminating
a bag boy for negligence confiscating smock without a
word of rebuke or advice attaching
honking sounds to the document gives it the kind of urban
authenticity clients crave ancient technology even if we're
relatively new caterpillars building fuzzy tent house
in peach tree to see if we can get away with it

that some Dutch bastard has trampled my corn

I inherit Italian money
and attain enlightenment Doctor Goat
      puts on his coat
          and goes out to make a call
               Kant
     at five-two nonetheless
          never lost a jump ball one of the great
            East Prussian leapers he
and before our replacements are brained and swallowed the
languages swerve into lexical byways that make our poor old
petitions unintelligible to all but specialists the
problem with tricks requiring trained kittens the damn things
turn into mopey cats too soon after all that almost impossibly difficult
education you're left on the street trying to extract a mark's silver
dollar with an animal that grows into and out of itself in the time it
         takes to remove its turban

if you're wearing my letterman jacket who are you then if not me
passing for younger in semipro football is all about states' rights

Does this cardigan make me look druggy the astonishing
　　　　　appearance of a bilge pump atop the town gazebo that
was an actual question by the way the floor is heaving this
　　　　　seems a plausible end it's shocking the number of
kids these days who don't know Latin but expect jobs
　　　　　anyway the great alphabetizing bonanza's
winding down these robots will have us sleeping
in the streets by next week looking for voiceover work in certain parts
　　　　　of those hills just whisper the name Campbell and the gunfire starts
　　　　　showing up as tiny umbrellas on Google Maps

and if we could get a vegan ashtray
along with those daiquiris that'd be
sweet thanks Curley

We the bulging bodiless eyes between fence slats viewing
auction items brought in a slow cycle before noumenal bidders bark
                    orders to trees
every new orange-juice morning these midcareer gouaches exemplify
                    promise unfulfilled the desperation of the cheesemonger's
                    son to take its place among daughters of long-
                              term commercial rent I
          don't remember meeting you here or walking
                                        away in the middle of an utterance are you
sure you haven't confused me with another of your speakers I'm the one
          who invaded Norway to show them what we do to minor languages yes
there had to have been a final
          pterodactyl to whose
                    memory it's perfectly OK to
                              pray like a silent letter practicing
                              valve trombone

                    this is gallery art okay it's about identity theft it's
                    recorded in obsolete video formats they have to fly
                    a guy from Bulgaria to run it that too is recorded
                    in discontinued Kodachrome and pressed into ingots

Turns out there's no mathematical way to
                    graduate sorry the apartment
            was taken the moment you gave notice the cat
        is gone Bob set it free which is stupid it had
never been outside these three rooms but there you go in
        retrospect we should never have commissioned that coat of
arms made too explicit our goal of regional domination the picked-
                clean bones of a priest of this parish and no one's seen him
        since Wednesday bingo the first rigged election the first
table more an outcropping with inadequate grass cushions this is
                    impure assertion of territorial sovereignty easily breached pastel
        diorama of myself being arrested for graffiti equations and
                    garment trafficking searchable brain vocab database just
            shards of syllables emerge to attach themselves to fond
spark ogle the otherness of presentation graphics include bouncing-
                    ball sing-along briefly inspired has passed
            this way toward one or more
        asteroid migration sleeper-hold tenancy
    dispute resolution pass-fail college course after-party cave
    rat stewed and raw a thousand counted
            years go boo blanket amnesty stirs habitants from
                multicentury hedge works

Hippias Major's a disputed dialogue because Socrates
keeps kicking Hippias and calling him a motherfucker is
considered more a mid-fourth-century thing

why it is hard to find the best Apollinaire translation
to use in a direct-mail campaign selling fundamental-
weighted market-cap exchange-traded funds and why
someone other than me is endowed with final decision-
making power in this regard

Little birds darted and bathed in dust the boy
clearly had PTSD the anesthesia-free
operation on the leg he almost lost his father holding him down no
wonder he found golden plates in a hillside people drank
a lot those days even ardent Jesusers as cicadas
emerge from their seventeen-year underground adventure they
head instinctively toward the
egg-and-beer batter and fly themselves thence to
drums filled with boiling oil delicious almost
unendurable the pastries sent over by mafia providers
can't be refused because the threat vague enough to be plausible that
you will be responsible for the aria of someone else's
pain includes two animated shorts and a newsreel confusingly
bleeds into feature through awkward infant
consciousness first bite of deep-fried bug our speechifying
capabilities center on ethos and pathos you want
logos go find a shopfront Armenian

oh slow the before-breakfast crowd of herdlings mass
anticipation of eggs sucked straight from chickens
while melted butter leaks from floors above

Apparently thrown clear the public-service
            pumpkin one's awakening body poked by
ghost of Maytag repairman from within the bus's gnawed fender our
            passports play telepathic mind poker while
UFO police reach within our folds if necessary will continue
            on without us take jobs as teachers in
small towns forget they began their existences as shredded
            documents somehow to come together using mirrors
and mathematics to conjoin brains continue a shared
            nameless consciousness subjective ten years
within five minutes of what we call real
            time what do you think do you want to invest

he who is entrepreneurial these midges bedevil those
who hideously besmirch the good name of their Cosa
Nostra forebears by teaching the young attend to their
lessons in a heap of partnerships soon severed

its caftaned mentor gesticulating in a way that holds
as though at bay entropic embassies approach

There's a long list of criteria for use in the selection process the
ship leaves Earth on what we call Thursday if you're not
            on it you've been judged inferior by the committee or
didn't meet even the low minimum requirement for consideration probably
        a genetic thing you should just go back to work this is good
            in the long run it clears your mind like ammonia you'll
    see right through camouflage to the reeking
                            pipsqueak hiding there are mortal consequences
for absence in the leaves there are more garlics than most folk
        are capable of imagining some are purple some
    hold jobs as violated sentence boundaries others
            in the southern hemisphere have taken to trees
with squirrels and perform the ritual confusion of who owns rent
        from the particular alms bucket dug from the ruins
            of Western metaphysics a field of poppies row on row

Plato was gargling when I asked him about what Socrates
liked to eat as a kind of test because I knew the answer was
canned spinach

I think therefore ascribing consciousness
to ourselves a form of anthropomorphism

Cuthbert here is the vigilance officer
on this planet he can inspect the rest of your crew for ticks hours earlier
the guard dog felt the pinch of the tranquilizer
dart in its thick neck the analogy trudged
on in shame
false
explanatory awakenings spread nut butter on bare
air
the versioning is off the risk-adjusted returns need a fluffer pronto the
same carny what thought up the bogus zinc cold
remedy now sells eggplant skin cancer cures in the sunburn belt as a
kind of retirement piety is it or pie-eating contest view of
humans they
don't yet know how to score big with all these
harvested preferences cute as bugs rolling around in multicolored
jumpers the truth is writing and deploying these programs mean
jobs for folks who buy soap from corner stores proprietors of
which then feed brown lettuce to the
kid chained in the basement grows
up to tend the fighting chickens so
everybody wins

people coming from the university to measure distances between competing vernaculars

Some sort of sorting mechanism left out in fog to get wet
autoerotically on the fire escape the blinking stork believes its luck still
clenching days later the beanpole sales rep
hits head on hanging fixture is a lawsuit waiting to grow up
and start a family of local ruffians are
friendly enough when out loping snared
with other similarly flummoxed
gopher goners Epicurus' argument of nonexistence not the emotional
panacea he portrayed even then the walk from gardened plot
to Stoic porch an allegory of nonconsolation logic's
logic it's the authority of explanatory wounds that wobble oddly on the
downslope from carousel to bowling alley the
examples have started their own
fellowship society complete with
sash and pendant fez and wand

it is either hylozoism of my way a highway either
panpsychist jerked prechicken or ex nihilo presto chango

Once the mirrors have been corrected the images
             of ourselves as gargoyles come clear oh you can cry or
you can embrace and celebrate a future
             life of frightening children on their
ways to controlled meritocratic distribution but choosers
             can't be beggars I've seen it happen I've embraced
       it as bum life retractable thumb razor thud
of regime change across town July the days grow shorter ears
             of hares retract at stench of martyrs moving overland
to colleges in fields the language puffins
             grow dark in chant whole hamlets held
together with snot the upper-respiratory mortar god
             gave Murray to make Ike and work him

you're free to light out for unincorporated districts if you think
you can find any invisible-hand package stores will trade you
bourbon for the feral cat skins you manage to harvest at great
physical and emotional cost then be the guest

in clothes that are almost dry the originator the creator the
impresario of this folding theater on the run ladies and
gentlemen the cousin of Gary Busey the actor

Friends fall through floors time bends in gravity a
weak force allows galaxies to wave to each other it says here skins
crawl up walls have messages on them my
childhood dream of becoming a successful hobo dead
till I looked in the shiny toaster one day the whole goal
has been plastic landfill pole
to pole bacteria that eat it will rise to replace
us and travel to other worlds this back
when the Bronx had trailer parks and cabbage farms you
understand Esperanto but you don't do much to flavor
it in succession a chronicle of sudden invisibility one day go
from opaque to semitransparent then gone

junk mail and noise pollution corporate identity
theft a pleasure to meet cattle on the way to Golgotha
Springs an ancient retirement haven for booth workers on Judgment Day

empty eye sockets on conference panelists when
heads swivel toward your entering presence you drop the sack
of millet and can't run

That's some thoughtful librarianship right there plenty
of pudding for Bodhidharma came from the West to
get to the other side to
swim in money means to reckon its viscosity everyone
I knew was in Pandemonium for selling stolen babies to dogcatchers we made the
most of it we hosted potlucks it seemed important
that the servants take piano lessons to
defend our compartments against fiends and
that is precisely the wrong thing to say to a Menshevik in a shattered clinic

here is the public explanation become the work
itself requires four giraffes
in engineer's caps running without pattern across amplified plywood

to prefer a varnished truth a nicely glazed verity an opalescent
patina on the bubbling fats of gnosis

Mistaken belief that bottom sheet has been torn apart
by sharp toenail boat having floated with me in it away
from relative's private berth to encroach on ocean rights of hostile neighbors a
series of brothers cannot be enticed to assume
responsibility for the carve-off despite the monthly $30 stipend angry
telecommunicational art brut corridor a
resilient baby doesn't mind being dropped on a small dog with beautiful
long red-blond hair and a nonresonating yip no it's
not my dream you say while trying to push me into traffic
near The Cloud of Unknowing Public House a treasure
trove of fungi lore is this even ever enough this not bliss tattooed
above raw wrists emerging in the
din of early evening commerce a fat fin these
the legitimate goals of the completion portfolio
itself an aspirant in the burly universe of retirement scenarios gone oddly
wrong you need to sell this to a dozen or so
people a week just to stay afloat in the cutthroat unworld of multiplayer
gaming paraphernalia sits still on shelves of brick in cupboards of
vanishingly few respondents take lime with the tic medication

where we come from there's no language at all just words
for things and long descriptions of vehicles
               wiping out at Dead Man's Curve

You've got your doughnuts you're walking into the desert
    along a pretty good road you have some sort of open safety pin
    sticking into the small of your back your hands are invisibly
fastened to abductor muscles there's an orange car almost on the
                    horizon Dinah Shore is in it
pop-eyed in cartoon heaven the drunkard leads his flock to the consulate
    doors a high and almost inaudible
            whistle understood to host trillions down
the hill near the water a girl and pet gull draw equations in the sand
of this idyll the bills seem to have piled up in our absence but who is this
    we you speak of hesitates before the shining puddle

                    they'll lend you their paid-for camera and upload
                    the architectural image to their cheesy site then charge you
                    triple whether the crime is solved or not the infant convinces the
                    child tricks the adolescent into helping it seize power

all titles had to be changed to explain
the tailed children alive within the bush attracts
eloquent bees to its flowers and eats them

Virtual reality program that simulates or
so you keep telling yourself the experience of
studying for the Chinese imperial examination for years in an
unheated shed and then failing and having to cart bricks
till you die hasn't really yet found its
audience you
need a dermatologist to look at that spot price index wraps
around entire numb side of post-stroke body double
walking tour of concourse up creek to alien
word horde the steam
bath or table and predictable population
bomb detonated on some future Tuesday ahead of
tech fix in its wood-meadow borderland pacing
off repetitive narrative of predation

way I heard
the story the grasshopper eats the ant and spends a cozy
winter wrapped in felt sipping fine wine

babies
almost always choose the cooperative puppet

Upon successful completion of the public
oral defense but before the conferring of the actual degree the
candidate traditionally works for
several years selling cigarettes in a Winnipeg
nightclub old-fashioned cigarettes old-fashioned
nightclub Luther
from death fear Calvin
from suspicion of incompetence as a humanist
is someone produces a new edition of an old book

space school involves the slow turning of gnomes

evangelizing next to Woolworths the truly
competitive beetle will forget it's in a race and
just head for daylight trusting imagelessly there'll
be a meal on the other side of bettor exhortation

And the shit keeps on coming our main product the
            agent of our dim-glimpsed *telos* a pile a mighty
mile high the real clay from which Eve fashioned Andy the penalties
        for age-related miscalculation grow with an arbitrary severity the
                    fiendish Thatcher would have adored chewing
            off this last strand of membrane to go
under to submit to the knuckle to read
            from Ephesians to send an arcing spout above the
                    dump adjacent but generally downwind
in relation to financial concentration plants
            may be animals without brains doesn't
                        mean they're not people we
            find only nine goony
guys at the center we smite them and
                    roast their shoulders it might've been nice
to have us some rice and maybe some navy beans we sang
        and sang as the hurricane wiped its ass with our
                grandparents' built environment back when
computers had a lot of wires that came like snakes alive

your dentist needs to know your religious
affiliation so your family can be billed appropriately for the
burial of your teeth

                                                    Purged
                        from the official history of the universe shaped
                                        like a knot of fake flesh
                        about to be eaten by a catfish you
                        robot janissaries will solve a lot of personal
            problems for the ultra-high-net-worth segment the soul
whether in man or in animals is not in fuzz
            or in hair we are not causes of our own predestination let
            all professors conform to these prescriptions this is not
            just an admonition but a teaching that we impose François
                        de Burgia Jesuit 1586 your job is to
                        very slowly fix the elevator as a
            dilettante of life's stranded moments I set
forth to earn a modest fortune cajoling a fuel agent for
transit to the raw edge of mainland so often glimpsed from the
                        slats of this vassalage

                        admire the crew cuts and badges of these young activists
                        steaming buns for the hungry against Danelaw injunction

protein is protein and the god that lives
on the edge of the clearing a very wicked weasel

Mrs. Potato Head version baby
potato heads funny uncle potato head the distant cousins upriver we
were there at close of world confined to quarters intermittent
intercom system still sputtering sputters into
ears gone red from rubbing in that contraction infographics appear and
vanish rapidly on hides of precedent tenants I refuse
the offer of a spray-on tie before entering
the banquet would have involved climbing the stairs to the
bedroom of my fiancée's parents in ancient
Greece those were terrible days in Alta California the police
chiefs ran wild the purposeless youth chewed
bark to ease pain of bones broken in impromptu
demolition derbies the whole bad
idea of jokey TV weather reporting just then emerging from the lowest
rung of vaudeville you should calm down it
is the Albanian way to accept one's
self-made fate it's a whole sub-
subdiscipline the study of parts how wheels fall off when they hit holes

decades centuries later letters
separated into words allow
transmission of interests into vaster
pleats of universal clerisy

Banks are living things with lungs codicils entrapped
scandal photos of course they get to vote early in the vast migration a
mighty blowable horn sprang from the guts of
amortization we were off to the stars or a new
new Héloïse named Jamie an
angry scrap-metal dog
guard has arrived at your attention I'd
turn and leave briskly for the cloudbank out
the side door it's a DANG cold morning in
Hell Marshall or Marshal if you wouldn't mind edging over a little
closer to the noose this won't take long I'll
personally send your widow a chunk of your mustache in
fact I'll deliver it myself you're
not on the short list the long list the longer list or even the longest
list so oil up and get ready to dive a DURN cold morn in
Hades Sadie I don't recognize any of these technicians I'd
draw you a picture of the town square we sleep in but they'd
shoot me as a spy if they saw me do it doesn't
know its way around a semicolon just spurts banner heads likely to
increase opens and click-throughs salutatorians
need not apply this is a buyer's market we don't hire runners-up maybe try
Costco whatever that is

the shooters have all been identified as property-rights
enthusiasts arguing their plan to convert land to hyperland with
dark matter bombardment and dimensional slippage if I
read this ticker rightly

Doctor Goat put on his coat composed of Christ's
wounds and went out to make a call affecting not at all the
powerful codes working together to give other
codes ontologically distinct caricatures of their own profiles people
are sacks of themselves the principal announces at assembly wind
and rain whips the few high dirty
windows of the gymnasium the tuba player clears
her spit valve a janitor that's me lurks under the stage people are sacks
of themselves and flickering disco
pantsuits of others the principal announces as Doctor
Goat arrives to lead her off

but in Alberta found only the kettledrum
serfdom of King Sugar Beet sense that these bankers will
shoot if fucked with

and so to the end of the paved
                    universe come all of us to shed our names the
finches for whom it is always lunchtime

       It's not just that I've forgotten the password but that it
can be shown never to have been logically able to exist in the first or any
subsequent place so the purchase is denied the feet skitter on inclined
gravel whose slender mutations over time can be charted with stick figures
and twine my teeth come jangly loose on kneepad trip up length of bleachers to
                    be inspected by work boss's underling that
you were born among the thousands of shellfish generations does
not in itself enhance the moral standing of your claim your claim
       just stands there is a local
                    ghost employed to scare off hikers every
                              person on Earth at some point last year or
so it seems received by mail a clock in a box about four inches by four by
six weighing thirty pounds *bigod!* what kind of material has such density has to
be hooked up to a television and requires adjacency to some sort of small shrub
your life springs forth as images spiraling into a series of canceled infinities explain
everything you need to know about the celebrity waiter

                    to convince the tenant he knows me I point to the floor
                    warped by the last flood and say Remember

grown fat on the mineral-
rich tears of Gilligan forced to kiss a younger taller cleaner-
shaved version of myself and then comment
on the experience for Italian television

Streamed live just a start to enlarged communication
paradise bullpen the danger dinner that it might
speak all the millions
I made as a tennis umpire gone the chowder confiscated my very
name and sex changed in a Malebranche instant the
little donkey and I set off on what was
thought to be deep experienced-based
insight now exposed as self-satisfied rentier calculation larded
with delicious veins of cobalt blue low-Calvinist blank I would
bet on the angriest beaver to win the fight a lot
of off-road mudding ends in carbon monoxide tragedy is
nature's way of saying Spinoza's secret
name before bowling strike the almanac
predicted intergalactic war for today isn't happening unless it did and
that accounts for the sudden disappearance of nickels

who is Hoover to have refused
a dog as gift from Paraguayans but
kept the cat Colombians meant him only to pet

that's it you get one t-shirt for the week don't come
crying to me if it stinks early you can go to church
covered in molasses I've seen it done

They put small objects in drawers you have to open
and that is the exhibition which is also cinema derives from the art
of pulling without breaking you know those people
who stand from the audience and speak their minds in rambling ways at
conferences and other public meetings well you've
become one of them we'd like to record what you say
and play it back for you at seemingly random intervals to gauge your
reaction with electrodes that's the thing that's
it right there we like to pretend we've turned up places on purpose but
it wears thin my friend told me that in fact Father
Malebranche does not believe that there are bodies a principle of
interpersonal physics you're correct your very existence
is an embarrassment is exactly what makes you the greatest
opera singer of your half-generation

just as a contractor feeds his horses
only the finest oats so too do my
shirts receive the ripest boysenberries

best to confess your grandsire a halibut and we can exit
sequester and be home for last prayers

Can you describe the man was he wearing a wool hat was that
wool hat my hat was it possibly anthrax do you need a moment
to collect yourself from your night job buffing
floors at the dealership I'm pretty sure they
tortured me in my sleep and used a machine to wipe out my memory of it they
renamed me Colleen and set me up in bakery
work which I did till I convinced myself they weren't
looking and ran off that took nine years goods
and services lumped together but wrongly thought of as different baby
zebras entire kingdom of numbers and
buttons breaks down when it recognizes its own preposterous
indeterminacy the many syllables of the dog's treasure an
excavated bone your name
systematically encased in shit dries
on the roof of a perfectly ordinary
building of the late nineteenth century applies
for work to supplement meager pension why
are there bed bugs instead of nothing I say resembles
the image cluster volunteering for KP to avoid
having to socialize with farm boys weep
easily when they stop to think

a terrible disappointment to one's international
baccalaureate professor has shingles

you're never more than seven feet away from a spider
predicting the weather pointing at swirly charts joking
with the traffic cricket all in this sordid pasturage beyond the cave

There is no subjective experience of time groceries
bought with bizarre scrip of our bishopric you yourself somehow
become international default currency a unit
spoken aloud standing in the shrinkage of form the
rumor that memories of
human meat monkeys float
in jelly tanks in aft compartments tended
tenderly by beautiful immortal sentient human robots is
false no practical means of storing memory of that
sort has ever been found the ships plunge
on like rats up drains massive
piles of leftovers no
way they'll all fit in the tiny fridge whole cooked peahens mound
after mound of baked ziti great pools of poached
abalone apricot compote slivered ham living
wire tunes non sequitur to discursive
failure yells at motorists possibly a
hallucination or hoax eventually
these rags must be gathered and washed and redeemed returned
to their habitats their earnest works the secretly
jubilant corners of unnamed spacetime glow
hungrily for constables to ruin symmetry

thus the stupid love dolphin too cheap to meter

A surprising number of revelations not just Hubbard's occur
during dental procedures this needs to be investigated
objectively with double-blind research protocols and secret
infiltration of the hygienists' guild taps wrist
where watch would be if there were still watches to indicate the
session's now over he's on
silence and it's time to pay up sprinkled
with shiny dust the bird I think possibly a common robin flies in a
window Xtianity begins in Anglo-Saxon
Britain beautiful immortal sentient human robots assemble knots
of conscious postdigital equilibria amid the
vast mauve expanse of almost nothing

hen-tooth details of Tillman frag a
transhistorical fact of planting culture

here in my final Irish castle I crave possum
served the old way in cups with drizzles
of raspberry vinegar and a hostage tied up next to me eyes
bulging at the antics of my pet starling Roger

Though both are infinite the set of exquisite
poems composed by a subsystem of beautiful immortal sentient
human robots our descendants is larger than the
set of words in their glorious dictionary to which thousands of new
entries are added each microsecond syllables
from crashing minds of
ancestors decorate the aural sphere of each
ship intergalactically proceeding amid
rehearsal and recombination of textured subhistorical configuration fuel
the momentum of these our descendants the beautiful
immortal sentient human robots some
standing less than a micron others more
than a kilometer when fully unfurled

little of our marketing work these days involves the slaughter
of animals though there's one door next to the utility room that won't open

of all the giant beasts that thudded in despair across the megacontinent this one is your substitute
teacher writes its name on the board in unknown script and turns to point a quivering digit

They try to speak through teeth of lost
cocaine clan flaps in barbed wire funnels
                                    appear in air as though guided by robot
shark with hat in back seat watching plans hatched in front still alive
long past junior college which was when most folk died
                    in the old days shoving bodies into
                            crevices between boulders that's you told those
British bastards say the postcolonial object an
        illegitimate Netherlandish fellow has
                    somehow managed to step all over my maize who
                            will eat whom in the coming hot and cold a
question perhaps best left for the new geographers understand
        where the chutes will be placed given the all-nude review
            of literature too late now the gates thud shut on toes
                    and fingers ended up here through the agency of
                            shuttles that are themselves the point

I like these tips for living the void sends us flowers
of its research program needs funding like any other
sect spreading devotional tracts by hand among extended neighbors

Bento's anathema I'm guessing stood him well
in the pool hall known as sexual floor polishing is
a practice thanks for networking here's your bagel

I admit I'm a bad Mormon I smoke LSD and
                    drink forbidden colas in Satan's pajamas but
I have blood relatives were handcart pioneers moved
                        to Canada to live the principle so you've
                    pretty much got to give me your stew later some
                    impulse passed angered
badgers back and forth instead of snakes combining antinomianism with
        paintball entrepreneurship not a whole lot else
                to do in those northern clearings I need to add
                        a definition of hurdle rate to the glossary then we can
have our nice little chat and so arrive at the end of an arbitrary
        sequence having been utterly transformed without
                noticing the elderly mouse can barely
                        round the corner Prometheus
                stole nuclear fuel rods from gods to give to North Korea now
        the universal donor's chained to rock while Dr. Oz
tears open his guts to feed his liver to Oprah

no roof-caught fish could taste as sweet as this
slender eel of the subbasement

Moving pictures typically attract certain moth
species and repel others find solace amid crumbling
statues come to life and order coffee it's a simple
     test of short-term memory if you flunk you're
     thrown out with rest of the trash relax and enjoy
     the process starting now I wear a disturbing hat
on hot sunny days the duck I'm guessing will be adopted by
soldiers store the plastic chips in a vast bowl for God's great
glory it's brittle cold at project's end the tools gathered and
     twined for transit downriver to next hamlet
     needs a secular exorcist it is a living in
pimento fields the olive-stuffing works attached go back
     before monotheism so be on time look alert answer
     when poked
     manifest form's a
     scratcher and biter Einstein skeleton used to scare
     birds away from crops in advertising

so templated over the evidence of trepanation can't come clear for eras

There you go again confusing
                    corpuscularianists and itinerant acrobats Senator the year
            is not 1669 and you are not the twenty-three-year-old Gottfried
Leibniz whom I knew when we were both freshman
                    Ohio representatives Gassendi
            could easily have pinned Descartes in
                    Greco-Roman though freestyle's
                            surely another matter you'd
    think bookcases and books emerged in tandem but
no the former preceded the latter by
                    several confused centuries it's a texture thing the
            royal road inevitably unpaved toward morning the up-
                            sloped curve in brush land leads
                    away from twin villages into
            scratched-photo patches of local
        pseudo blueberries

carried off by thousands of their stout workers to underground
caverns measureless to Sam remembers that
Sonny Liston wrote his master's thesis on Comus

Time machines were people once and will
be again when enough pilgrims have
circled them and paid toll new visual
acuity melts thin walls raptures small
mammals technological artifact
once a wonder now retired to museum's annex or stored cold for spare
display parts that's some fine superficial analysis right
there a sparrow pops up goes haywire in dust bath given
cursory glance by nut-crazed squirrel must bury
horde before winter felt somehow to be
coming you say copywriter I see from your portfolio
you mostly write captions do you think you could
write an essay to get my kid into Dartmouth is the only real job
I have to offer one day's work five hundred dollars start now how
can there be a cop in the house if the house
doesn't exist answer he's not a real cop he's
pretending so he can get something to eat like the rest of us

bit of tape adhered to table decades
later still there finally picked off as flakes after what
has to be counted a massively successful career

associate degrees collected in my
wandering quest for annulment I'm ready to start work
at first wiggle of a foreman's tentacle

Some future squadron learns
        intricacies of turning left on parade no reason
        to think at this point you could have been anything
other than what you are a comforting style of determinism for some an
        outrage for others the images tending to blur together the
        porridge not near hot enough to please a bear
           of my girth and renown just
try opening files last saved in 1994 the beautiful
        coils unfold in real time or folds uncoil thus
the revolution served the terrible spankings Rousseau dreamed of face
        on floor and ass in air the long and necessarily walked
        distances between cities those days you
           have the wrong person of the same name
who has never heard of Wilfredo and his troubles persistent
        memory of arriving at a public beach
and looking for a place to sit down and think about a person
of the same name crashing through a guard rail of some sort tiny
        people and animals darting to burrows
as the bicycle makes its pained ascent to be publicly stripped
of one's duties after the lease expires a gondolier appears
        to hold the book aloft and cackle

a sort of Deleuzian cleaning service that also evaluates boy bands can
stand on the rim of a potential event and tease it into implosion these
scraps of laminated posters all that's left

From now on all my friends are going to be thermal
fluctuations choose us randomly to run kiosks at strategic
                  intersections in an infinite universe Mark Twain
      and Clara Bow are worshipped as rival messiahs constantly
                        disappearing within hollow mountains but
eventually you're in single digits everywhere you look like
          a handsome monkey and smell like the delicious charred
                  edge of a deep-fried magnolia the data-
crammed spy ball batted over the playground fence to an espionage
        confederate nonchalantly bends to snag the slow roller drives
                        off in a van but I've been seen
having to go north to find a southern turnaround peopled with syrup-
            sipping yellers ought by now to have been made
                  soporific in mud-spattered borrowed clothes at
                  high-tide pole but I've been seen

I failed a Turing test at work was sent home early hey
in outer space we're talking sister cities in the literal sense long
                              painful grunting births of trillion-
                    cabined satellite megalopolises if
              you can imagine them you already live there I
     failed the Shroud of Turin test in
     rooms largely open air that
Aldo called an apartment in a city melodramatically from which
              one could not return after arriving by roller train

Harry Morgan born Bratsberg has sex with a dog-faced man in an
episode Webb showed only at Kiwanis smokers

if your name has three W's you are a witch my friend congratulations
on the wonderful little dog's signing bonus

Dread packet fermenting on ledge
of dimensional information booth unstaffed at this
early or late hour a distant sweeper disappears
behind heaped bundles a great kidder this
quiddity says what do you get when you extract a rabbit from the
scene of its ardor no peeking the idea of
testing is to systematically
exclude lurkers looky-loos wee lambs half-sentient air
conditioning subunits and anyone else not native to
Athens and its surrounding agricultural heritage belt having
hauled this hamper
from SRO rooms to sublet apartments to improvised
lean-tos for decades now no I'm not going to let you
use it in your welded assemblage unless you give me a
hundred dollars right now just for thinking about it

its underside addenda almost
illegible in agate type

if I forget my new-bought pair of
pants on the counter when do they become abandoned property available
to anyone willing to build a defensible shed atop them

I can rewrite those banner ads to reanimate your parents rise
from disastrous holes to worship the toga of Æthelbert cisterns
from which steams hiss the crackdown when it comes
will be sold as love punches sense
that all devices provoke the same static effect block or obliterate stream
of enchanted data Baudelaire always imagined his
reader about to drop book and run off without
quite registering the last line of any characteristic
flaw of opals
assigned individual alphanumeric series based on our predetermined
intelligences and trustworthiness given a nudge out the door told to get
into the middle lands and elsewhere to sell subscriptions through
screen doors that's actually how you attain enlightenment you become
the screen door and then they call the sheriff

children fear parents
are unstable realities turns out they're right to worry

Well now that's your problem right
there said Doctor Goat pointing
to the final bit of Gottfried's harmony proof in Latin all the bent
bits look like god parts feet
wrapped tight in paper towels rifles pressed to shoulders out here early
morning we pay for our own bullets the state of Maine buys the chow doesn't quite
capture the exponential burnt rubber smell that
renders the animal unconscious for tagging upon
waking runs through the appearance of a chute
and up a grade to vague grassland all a hologram ninety-
five percent of everything is bad but 99.9999 percent of everything is doomed
to pulpy amalgamation Dinah Shore is in it

Oh you think it's possibly not over you are obliged
by your very angle of perception to think and believe it's not
                        over but it's over although as it turns out in the next
                                episode that's not at all the case Stan and Ollie
are chased by a bear into a spooky house in which nudes recline on
                        piles of ripe peaches the franchise is open for business this
is not over the rich
                        are in the middle of deciding what
they'd be willing to trade in exchange for continued privilege it turns
                        out not much they think they've got a seller's market
in tiny concessions I see the queen of England struggling
                        down Beadel Street in a walker I say hello she turns and
                                spits hits only her favorite corgi

                        phenomenal what Husserl could get up to in a day while
                        others played cards on smoke breaks behaved otherwise like
                        silent-movie extras walking in and out of dry goods stores

Got a nice write-up on the town blog remembered
when you was just a lout pulling an applecart the hill on Trout Stream for its
grandfather half goat had you penciled in for a 10 o'clock the mundane
medical procedure performed robotically in connected centers building a
database for eventual liftoff don't
speak walk away turn a corner quickly duck into stairwell leading down
to door opened by guy smoking slip inside scramble through confused
warehouse area to vent leading down into tunnel goes a quarter mile to
other side of bridge sunlight and safety whew
travelogue narrator on heavy beta blockers would be disqualified from all
Olympic shooting events except the new assault rifle demonstration sports and
possibly the tank relay what's
eating you folks used to ask at first sign of gloom lifting pint
or highball to fuzz outline of that with which it is mandatory to reconnoiter

hypothesis that these torn bits of paper can be
reassembled long enough to prove gravity the pious
fraud we've always suspected

Hand-packed in the juice god gave it on the day of
reenactment thinner than syrup less
evaporative than benzene wrapped
individually in red leaves/leafs it
is all energy
burned conserved transformed sent halting to
preschool move market through funnel sow
confused belligerence among the temporarily unindicted saddlers and
trimmers of your infinity class pool so poking around city
archives have bribe gaps in the guts of arrogant Mob
marriages force aldermen to
launder lucre from illegal codfish through Dominican bodega
circuit keeps average price of smokes down forty cents one
goes into the sensory deprivation tank a pimply sophomore filled
with vampirological lore emerge a decade later a vague pathway
communicating between two disputed sheep meadows one
loses one's attachments as one loses one's kitchen gadgets they
break or are eaten by goat medics or
dissolve along with their extensions

picture our heroine about halfway between Tautology and
Contradiction trying to hitchhike without thumbs

not just biographies but entire lived
lives reversed and altered by a single extragalactic
incantation pearled from the mud of this fake duration

You should learn to be an adult by looking at other
randomized adults do things for money merely
to seem plausible in the surveillance video your eighteenth-century
forebear appears clear as day to cast a rural hex it
may seem like jabbering to you but back
in the lab we'll pin up its flaps and
have a poke at its terrorist-harboring syntax it's
not fair to gauge
your interest in a subject till you've worn it
rotting around your neck for at least an epoch

operator get me the other operator to get me the supervisor to
transfer me to quality control

you just go on a couple of nerves you want a certain subset of
everyone to want to go to bed with your woodshop birdhouse

Coffee journeys south to north accumulating value we
used to call them shows now they're
appearances and their endings are disappearances into
hydraulic infrastructure beneath and around
cities you don't see the thin cable to which you're attached because
it moves out of sight when you try to
turn around quickly mirrors don't work controlled by
reflection patent no proof that any of these
Earthlings are sentient let us eat them we are hungry we are
angry at the contingencies that
led us here from our home galaxy so peculiar these time-
lapse origami figures every few hours propel fresh dung
at the screws every few minutes a reconfigured regret grazes in the
gunsight of half-consciousness reunion
planned among cabins pegs the image
of tactical retreat to the Arkansas peso buys itself
back in a complex hedge opaque
lake water strangely warm is alma mater first job
as journalist to retype dead
predecessor's article and fabricate quotes

Bart Simpson Scientologist Daffy Duck Mormon Betty
Rubble Satanist Olive Oyl Zoroastrian

Hypothesis does not predict a series
of discrete but related events culminating in a diagramed
                narration a technical term of art can be measured
        with this meter condemned to a rancid pit dreaming its lost
                fanged twin
hat of hammered tin and secret Vivian Vance undershorts are in fact the
        leash we gnaw on is what you're saying Daryl have you
                got a spare cigar for Mr. Dithers has become homeless
                        in old age you see one spider outcompetes
another spider is moral allegory a writ-small Masonic demonstration
                made vivid with husk and hull antique
camcorder differential docudrama vanity project smeared on lens equals
        about half of two monkeys in the famous typewriter room of
                them each century one in three thousand chance of
        asteroid destroying Cincinnati

the store has removed its products to the staff-only
sawdust sector behind a curtain of beads requires
you to describe the parts you want and then cooks them
for you while lecturing on the Bahá'í faith

On the lawn a timorous mammal with
     no discernable middle the house
          taken over by bad people who
               lay eggs and complain at the
bistro about being served food on a
     plank when the bare tabletop will do dog
     days enter annals with distant baying means
     the fox still has a chance if it can get organized and
          rent an algorithm lets it present a
fake self trapped at mouth of invisible acid bath below the
               hounds go tumbling Blondie herself
               goes back to college to get that long-planned grad
degree in logic one of her professors an extinct
     marine arachnomorph arthropod but here we make do
          with a bit of arithmetic we scrape off the bottom of pots appear
               in windows of our beaming memory robots the
prepopulated spread sheets colonize exoplanets through processes of spacetime
     diagram initiation obviously if it could be thought it could happen but
     thinking it doesn't make it happen that takes walnuts need
          decades to establish themselves next to immigrant carp
ponds of course that was a mistake you could see it in the eyes of the trapped
          wait staff angling trays around corners

I return the gull to its baguette and row off blinking in
mottled sun through leaves as though I can never not
depart this place and will always have been gone from
here already is the manifesto

the white keys indicate taboo within the discipline of
anthropology itself makes up for its lack of market discipline with
steep practitioner fees and occasional raffles

We are children married
children taking shirts off together in the past's future
to the rough surface of this planet
again and again the procreative mambo must be
witnessed to be valid architecturally I need
a provost I need a provost right now wrong
in the wrong way the answer a warm no from the
product chief dangling baited foot above trout stream a mirage none
theless have no idea who you are and
why you're trying to make conversation with them in the
contact zone between two parties of gathered
mourners oh you can bet the Vatican has a thick
file on you if you've ever so much as
walked by one of those suspiciously
pagan street shrines Hal
David and Rev. Moon in nonagenarian suicide pact shocks scholars
of American song and new religious movements these
numbers are random they are not
random enough Gestetner
as verb disappears with our liberty

*I am not properly in line the text
has not transferred from one apartment to the other
despite the damage deposit clearing I enter the library
holding hands with André Gide*

Young Joseph's heart was not yet pure enough to let him lift
and read the tablets trillions of so-called individual
consciousnesses stored in this tiny thumb drive hard to believe
all marching orders come from three universes over we had to
write sonnets in Spanish translate them into equations that is
how we learned we were judged arbitrarily and sent packing even
the fallen logs we sat on had signs saying no sitting this is
        not a government job its
abyssal certitudes channel ghosts
        of ghosts gone awkwardly over why do you
            think they call it dopamine in a dream
                preventing a chicken from being lit on
                    fire deposited as
guano on this tiny island hailing distance from the Bohemian
consulate the proposal that there's only the one long obscene word and we all
        spend lives barking part

a lot of time spent figuring out how to keep the goldfish alive
in the transparent boot heel long enough to impress potential Saudi investors

What's a lemma if it isn't
listed in the glossary the assumption is you
learned it in the course of compulsory military
service is a subsidiary or intermediate
theorem in an argument or proof a
sudden screeching rip half a borough long in the non-
metaphoric it turns out fabric of reality itself has out-
kooked you my friend its goony shambles a warning to
swarmed molecules considering the jump causality
aflutter in its dressing of gauze
resembles our emblem the hazelnut our
insignia the crossed G with a terminal
bowtie clamp doubling the antenna field the
pope's red shoes and ermine underwear at barter
auction post-apocalypse nostalgia items sell well in
living memory chorister Campion reports duty roster
defiled by rebel pheasants a nerve dies but the thumb heals

there's no reconciling some
antagonists you shouldn't try there's no
escaping fate as scab ref in the lingerie league

Wow you look great have you been logging we've
almost run out the clock on another narrated lifetime this
has been brought to you by the shadow cabinet in the
extension built invisibly beyond the duck blind you have
stumbled upon acres of secret barley some cultures consider
all luck bad the
latest scholium makes clear Mondays
are infinite in number just as each is finite in duration you fall
down once or twice in public people think
they've got the right to enter your hut and poke around at
things in an order you'd prefer not be compromised rent-
seeking conglomerates own concession of electrical
impulses through air to ear all this yelling in the park wait that
can't be right I just got here these muddy footprints haven't
even dried the holstered wrench awaits our intention paid to
act as though it doesn't shatter teeth

fine words do butter turnips I've seen it in France

Same town different clones ample undersea parking occult
gang in charge of council leads to rebuke by adolescent
inspector general fat living at the confluence of several
        streams of coerced labor seen repeatedly across
cultures tool-improvement regimes analyzed in network and
        process theories avoid equations in public forums the
        quality goes on and on before the barking
seal of approval dives under again in search of char dodging
space cones part of the experience is almost
falling off the icy roof before entering the dormitory to
        plant low-light versions of Earth ferns amid the
        clutter you say slobbish I say not excessively house
proud I will take your silence for agreement to rationalize
in this sense means to use surgery to make all limbs the
        same length of kingly measure employed to pace
        distances between pyramids or funeral mounds

sheep kept illegally in basements by Iowans pretending
to be Basque activists pretending to speak Chinook Jargon

understandably don't like me
hanging around their daughter with my pants off but she is not their
daughter and these are not my pants

There's some question how the chicken
            got in the bag in the first place the slanted
floor of the grandparental shack seemed too wispy
            to support an egg let alone a full-grown bag bird and
vexed celebrant possibly myself trying to set it
            loose before we're both accused of some sort of
            impropriety nude tumblers precede the lecture our storefront
            fellowship refines its position as the flower
of revelation unfolds as the petals of revelation fall
            and are gathered in urns the earlobe-
tugging frenzy can't adequately be captured on video each
spring new
            phenoms appear to run throw
                        field hit and hit with power the
detached testicle that has come down to us as cultural rally
            cap backward itself meaningless but offers up statistical
                        clarity a sense of residency false but compelling

Yes there's no excuse at this point one
          should have stopped picking at it long ago
as advised the thing's whole job's to grow
          to replace you without losing access
to your commercial band signals happened to my grandfather
          one day repairing radios the next
outside watching his replica do the same giant 3D
                    printers roam the hills spewing thirteen-
          story mixed-use buildings with their own doormen
and supers so lifelike you've got to quiz them half an hour before
          they falter eyes start to spin suddenly poof
gone look there they are two flights up adjusting a flag pole if
you have to ask you can't afford the antigravity
          treatment cord wire rubber or something coated long
thin thing poking into present with defunct intent hiding out
          so as not to have to attempt to explain a theory of
advertising that includes your bid

and the syntax of many children is what
drives green wasp after red

the anteater gave birth eighteen months after last
contact with its mate through a process known as foreign syndication

We need to start demonstrating the reality of electromagnetic
fields as early as kindergarten if we're going to compete
with the Finns and the Himalayan Tigers we're going to
have to shock a few little darlings to accelerate the
      education of the others the way you
          pay for pure research is tax gambling I can't remember
your name though we lived together three years in I'm
pretty sure a tree or if not then how to
         explain these diagrams third-
            generation copyright owners swim
               toward illusory rent horizons end in
      massacre the inevitable switcheroo it's
great that you get to live in a house even though you're
Catholic in my day that wasn't done even in
      Semaphore City which was lax

suit jacket on backward my underwear torn off by crows through a
hole in overalls this structure's what we call a teardown

I who drive an ancient Rambler onto the assembly wharf
in search of treasure have myself abandoned contractual permission
to sell empanadas in the viaducts finally held together only by
      colliery apparatus of yesteryear pulled down a
bare century later to harvest metal allows streams to again flow in their
natural manner through the barns of outraged truck farmers even we lifelong
      bachelors look back in astonishment at the number and vivid consequences
of our marriages the unaccountable and mismatched
laundries we will collect we will gather up our asterisks our
             little stars will guide us back to the pencil sharpener

perhaps Ted Danson about to do squats convinces me to buy street flippers but
nothing
just a ramekin of sauerkraut and two stolen knives

Jesus shoves me schoolyard
transformed from lime lines to steep-
grade desert rubble the bad thief headed for us with lemonade

Grown but still young people from childhood
all named Jane appear with
ancestors on a planet of modernist architecture and civic squares crossing in
front of you ignoring your bleeding gaze I
a freshman dazzle my professor with knowledge of names titles dates but am
led away long-haired among adherents of a rival
professor who assigns urban rat-maze
befuddlement as scholarly object it's
never too late to reenter the causeway's maw you speak of potential as though
frogs give it up freely in their croaking they don't belong in what we call
the parlor you need to take them to the
shed out back the sun emerges
from decades of horticultural neglect that's
a really bad sign you should see a vet

Who bred these bat-winged blinking
congressmen can please come and pick them up
after field hockey practice or suffer damnation when I
commented on various warehouse items I didn't
realize I was ordering them but here they are years
later vacuum packed and ready to eat or inflate on
Mars or a part of the Moon we'll pretend is
          Mars to fool rubes
off an alley by the overpass the humming
              cracking and occasional pizzling crescendo caused by mandated
                    data deletions going on all over the inner
                          planets ahead of invasion not sure
          how I won these medals must have been for attendance or
                  something I did in a fugue state every housecat
has a territory and an inner representation of the duties to its own
                          ravenous hunger dogs lack
          the representations but see something like themselves in
cartoon silhouette going from panel to panel in search of love

How long can food be left out
among the rabbits of the field before it's
illegal to sell to pilgrims this a matter of some
corporate urgency if libraries are going to compete
they've got to start stocking porn and charging for private
viewing booths it just makes sense a child reading
a picture book for free might as well be eating the
creator's brain or depriving an honest
hyena of its livelihood we
had to turn in our shirts that
was a sad day the post office had closed the year
previous in response to the fourth volume of
Creighton's history of the papacy complexity
later exploded out here upon googled earth the limbs will again
be fins if need be baggage piled high on ludicrous novice
travelers in pedestrian tunnel under Italian tracks

*till you've actually had the experience of being returned for store
credit I'll ask you to pipe down or leave the pub*

every surface sticky with quantum immortality and
post-junk conniption transcripts

Stand up and bashfully say something in-
      dictable I double dog dare thee to sit
          down wear your hat and read a
             pamphlet while the anthem plays I guarantee some
        schnauzer will tap your neck from behind with two
    tattooed fingers but why were you there in the first
place if not to perform the empty rites of fake patriotism is un-American as
pear pie and triple parenting is a funny way to show ownership of
            objects by laying them out on a table putting
             different-colored dots on them all then wandering
        down a porch and into a small yard surrounded by crumbly wood
fences complaining from time to time about a lost turkey just
    as people brick by brick and angle
by measured antenna build these gently
bobbing examples of vernacular architecture so too did
    sweating citizens sit to write the words
in all the books headed for the masticator through subterranean
chutes to the delta's peaceable but dispersed anonymity the
      Flemish mercers them to pay

I sang jingles in lieu of thesis but the rabbit
runs from pain not death and even that is an
approximation of the scene's terrible specificity

leap days are government scams man they're
all about mind control not so fast the clicker can't
keep track the mutations blur to form a fly-size Buddha attempting to address
itself to Rumsfeldian cartoon moon haiku

Look through both you and the train window to the very
kidney of the inverse square law this
is OK as a first draft but now you need to focus your claim tighten
the lede highlight the nutgraf frame your evidence refute a
counterargument end abruptly chanting equations in front
of paintings is excellent neoconceptualism as is spreading false
statements at the information desk is
something the whole art-loving family can appreciate a pie in the face and a
dangling eyeball professors enforce their own
brand standards they steward syllable movement all
the people walking around thinking they
own the view of the river are correct

most of that code got fried in the centuries between x = 1x and xy ~ ab²

Sociologist of the dead-ball era drafted to fill out
      line in pepper drill during influenza outbreak thundering
crunch of armless soldiers on the go tail risks and black
          swans get together for beer and horse shoes at the
country club a pattern of affinities visibly enhances the pond's steep exit
          strategy I can see out my cured eyes now not only feathers but
lice enduring their own secular partings and goings-forth the labor
of the laborers the work of the workers compelled to prance efficient
allocation of resources runs cover for structural
cupidity astonishing in scope you're usually expected to assess
validity of sequential logic no matter what solution you came up with they're
also on lookout for highly successful guessers you
think the query has been sent by pushing a mental button wait all day
      for an answer to have committed surrealism in one season
          of life and then moved on to the vice presidency we
          need as little of this
          sort of thing as possible and there
is no afterward there are cots for liberal political economists to
lie down and rest up for death at the end a syringe and a horoscope
attached to each I entered a wonderful world of sentient PDFs

does it hurt much to be translated into pulses aimed at likely spots
in the galactic neighborhood oh yes it hurts terrible

There's no complimentary shrimp dinner for wallabies
anymore the new manager ended that after looking at the cleaning bills and
so the cobbler never again left the city limits but expanded
within them till even today we live inside
his enormous transparent gut it's
not remembered what Dr. Goat did next or even in fact
whether he made it to his so-called call anyway what kind
of doctor walks door to door I'll tell you a hippie that's what but
they sell cleats for three dollars downtown if
I can find someone to fly me there in one of the
new orbs I hear whooshing but can't see who
are these gibbering fascist militants and who let them into our gym a
hell of books for loved ones to stare
at perpetual fog filled the thin cylinder
in which we lived for daffodils' brief season congregationally

Containerized shipping changed the fucking
        what do you mean by world you commie.

      •

Feel my heart throb in weird knob at back of head
            seat of soul–not mine
      but that of a miscreant traveled interstellarly
via metalight and dug in for the duration
        at some point of seventies adolescent stagflation.

      •

Rob of old tells of Lloyd's glorious immolation on the pyre of Eros.
I remember church or rather
the fact that a memory has reiterated itself through
           years of mutations does not make it
important beyond the community center at which it is permitted to shower or the
        shelters among which it rotates.

      •

This the only remnant of Bo Peep, sliver of wrist bone.
Dr. Goat had it all along but his nephew let shrine archive
           workers in to save what they thought best after the
           tragic shooting.
They also found notes toward an incoherent ontology
           pasted on the underside of chairs.

      •

Legitimate descendants of the original panel stand to gain.
           They're all tall. The luminous fish
by which their forebears gained their treasure
           sits up now implausibly, through cooked lips speaks.

      •

It's difficult but possible to think oneself atop the rocket all along
        and all the popes and marmots likewise
toned and elongated by forces make gravity seem a limerick,
accounts balanced on the apex of a billion converging trajectories.

                        •

Students and teachers address an imagined conclave of mavens.
The conclave has trays of fancy sandwiches brought in whenever it wants.
The program administrators are likely to give out false addresses
        and to videotape your visit to the water closet.
It's what they learned to do at the University of Paris extension at Utica,
final flower of Ramist theory in the Mohawk Valley,
official agent for a nonexistent yet nonetheless copyrighted
        process of returning sea parrots to the discipline of their communes
        (tattoos not allowed in Hell by order of Merv Griffin).

                        •

Oh it's so gross. Don't show me no more pictures
I don't not regret nothing. We're not parts
        though cleavable. There's nothing
up sleeves that can't not be not bought for time served.

                        •

That was my fucking dream then, to hula from Uclulet to Tofino
        unfilmed, yelling, kept cool by a series of fucking volunteer misters,
hydrated drop by fucking drop from a reservoir of fucking Tang attached to head
        just like a fucking astronaut, you get me?

                        •

I didn't say a word. I didn't judge you
        any more than I judged this intergalactic mayonnaise that needs salt.

                        •

The foresters have made their inventory ahead of the infestation.
Some of them are licensed botanists who can arrest you.
They've got glints of elsewhere in their brooches summery
emblems of dalliance dot their breeches.
Light bounces oddly off incisors from this angle.

•

Let's walk it back. It has to be about something,
        some unwobbling piglet attuned to bachelor-pad space noise.

•

In my father's houseboat there are many mushrooms.

•

They'd begin with barbed image or syllable gone haywire
        and uncouple their arguments from the sin of Noah.
Which was what? *Shoddy execution of contracted work.*

•

The units were band, tribe, nation, empire, holding company,
        though not all layers were visible from all cairns
        at all times by any particular habitant.
Their priests were regularly whipped for drunkenness.
This we know from surviving cartoons.

•

The mop is ticking. In the janitorial sublime
        a mountain blinks dimly at the end of a utility alley
        and all but the most disoriented swing-dance enthusiasts have dispersed.

•

Filmed de-trousering as prank declined in late teens as cream pies came in.

•

Some philosophers think it obvious that everything is conscious.
They win the argument as soon as you start yelling.
And those words and deeds, those wishes and vertiginous awakenings,
        are bundled together with others into collateralized debt obligations
        and traded to pelicans for aluminum.

•

We leave buckets of toothpaste foam behind in the rental.
Oh there're ticks out there waiting for you let me tell you.
They're on the butts of deer and in the ears of darting rodents.
They concentrate their liquor in tiny sacks that seem of vellum.
I've seen them in trance brandish banners of chaos, utter
        oaths against the state's permanent emergency.
You don't stand a chance in those corduroy britches.

•

Belmondo puked in my cracker bowl one time in Athens.
Or rather that was me pretending to be Belmondo in Toronto
        pretending to be Athens, which is the same thing.
Those Trotskyites mainly became Army barbers.

•

They had villages and traded fancy cloths,
        farming and hunting gadgets, whatever
        taste enhancers from far away and various
        kinds of oil, say, but never made the leap
        into high-yield infrastructure bonds is what doomed them.

•

I stood next to Mao at the urinal of the Globe Hotel in lower Cranberry.
I could feel his minders size me up as no threat.
The shills come out to trick reanimated uncles
        back in spats from leukemias and bullet holes.

•

No one those days thought to identify as venture capitalist.
Money guy might've been the term, or silent partner,
      or boss, or Mr. Orlando from Port Alberni.
You want to open a dry-cleaning operation, you need to talk to X.

•

If I had to attest provenance, I'd say it was always here
even before the Atlantic people arrived with winches.
You've got to consider chalk and drainage.
Standing water is no friend to corn folk.

•

One day you're a revered Kremlinologist and the next.
Area experts almost never adjust to new mafias.
They have 72 hours to pack office and vamoose.

•

The woman playing Goneril's got whooping cough
and her understudy's a twelve-year-old boy who just lost a front tooth
      to a croquet mallet in the lighting guy's backyard.

•

A vast Rosicrucian conspiracy
      just as it's always been,
        Descartes at its heart,
a series of small liberal arts colleges serving as dispersed base.

•

That's the mandate: There are only so many images,
so called, we can take with us to Andromeda,
only so many nickel-plated athletic trophies,
not to mention only so many podiatrists especially
since it's unclear we'll even have feet on arrival.

●

I became desirous, my mother having died,
of seeing foreign parts, especially Italy.
                                    – Milton

●

                              Happy to have unloaded those supplements.
Now they're the problem of the Swiss moon colony.
We rotate the role of Goldilocks so everyone gets a chance to eat
                         three porridges publicly.

●

Revenge is not a dish, but if it were, it would taste best
with a sauce somehow made of the things
you'd like to do to people in return for what they did to you,
and there'd be no need to heat it up.

●

Well if you ask me, the sun certainly *seems* to rise.
And it seems to me that to do that it would have to *intend* to do so.
And if it *intends* to do so and *does* it, it must be some sort of *engineer.*

●

I can't remember anything–just names, dates, lineages,
          perceived slights, awkward pauses, bad haircuts,
          descriptions of female uncles, cats leaving the room.
Spiritual entrepreneurs invest in arrangements of exploitation
          to secure the surplus value of enlightenment and,
          they tell themselves, raise all sentient boats.

●

Now duck fat, there's an ointment.
               Makes everyone look good, taste good.

●

Gnawed meat grows back on these magic bones.
The ice cream sandwich has seeds in the middle,
          revealed as secret Arctic plant.

●

Mingus, pretending to be a taller Bo Diddley, yells at Creeley.
I stand forth on the ottoman.
          My MC announces me.
                    I stand down from the ottoman.
                              The show is over.

●

The principal task of the village council is to maintain a sense
          of self that persists unaltered from day to day despite
          the overwhelming evidence emerging weekly from Iowa labs.
I tried to be a drifter for a while when young but never fooled
          a single polis, taken always for mere aspirant
          to be pointed toward agricultural labor hall.
Usually managed to set up tent too near a municipal sprinkler.

●

It's not clear how the roof of the house
          can be connected to a government sausage outlet
          in a failing underground mall. Is it magic?

●

I absent myself from the frenzy of the recitation.
My plan to reappear at the end as though present all along
          and thereby gain credits toward graduation.

●

You began your lecture with a quote from the wrong Sinatra.

·

Aristotle skinny-legged and beardless stood
        imitating a heron for amusement of his charges.
For every earwig plucked squirming from its path
another galaxy blinks apology to its erstwhile mentor.

·

But the tree is real and sings songs
        that don't seem at all to reflect facts of arboreal life
        but rather hint at the grim fates of lottery winners.

·

I can't decide whether the primordial is soup, stew,
        or vinegary gravy from the deglazing project of early life.
If the latter, a lot depends on cooking temperature
        and what got stuck to pan or grill.

·

                                But books—pictures in books
that alter when examined, change to doors
        whose handles fall off, eat up a lot of statistical space
        in the almost infinite or infinite because always further
        divisible pause in the dog's shiver of hopefulness.

·

It was cold in Hell. They handed out sweaters.
                We stood on an observation deck. A guy came around.
        Most of us wore empty holsters. Apparently
                        some sort of confiscation had preceded translation.
Nothing much moved. It seemed peaceful. A person
        with the gear and outfit of an electrical line worker
looked up, startled to see us, and disappeared
        behind a bush, rattle of his shaking head just audible.
It came clear we'd come in the off-season.

None of our benchmark measures stood up for themselves.
    We descended on rickety ladders.

•

My name's called in English over a loudspeaker.
The past will be there when you don't need it. Just cease to be
        the antiquarian of your own peregrinations, lost in tundra.
This sounds like advice because it's coming from a space ant of the same name.
This sounds like rainy streets but sounds are funny.
They like to repeat themselves for emphasis and storm off
        silently into predawn improvisation trying
        to look like a properly rehearsed skit.

•

                        For decades a small, fierce owl
has followed me around threatening to pierce my wrist
if I pass on the cipher to an unauthorized third party
in contravention of my contract, which by the way I don't
remember signing and could not have since I can't read
or write and lack hands, mouth, eye sockets, ear holes,
and any other orifice that could plausibly grasp a pen.
And do you know in all this time the owl has not introduced
itself or said a friendly hello or sent a holiday or
bereavement card, nothing.

•

Then in a terrible sudden all these messages started pouring in
        over shortwave or however the hell we communicated those days.
Crown Prince Timmy has drowned in a ditch and we are blamed
        for not having slapped and counted parking meters completely.
We knew we had to split into parts and never again gather
        in a federation that might be subject to random police sketch.

•

But as I begin
       to age out of the program
a fly appears in my annihilating gaze
       and now its cousin, also now ash
but somehow still buzzing, a miracle of persistence.

      •

Those of us who stared at the test pattern till farm report
       gained from our discipline an immunity.
We went to visit but found ourselves not home.
It's a powerful differentiator a marketer might declare.
A mere hair caught in the door blocked entry.
Most of us understood the newish properties of physics
but they didn't much affect our daily lives as rent collectors.
About that: I was an apprentice, so my only job was to
       collect rent from myself.

      •

Your subject-matter expertise evaporates.
            What can you say?
          That's what we came to witness.
An elevator speech by an actual elevator.
A pinhole of light from a close-by dwarf galaxy, mere
millions of stars just off the heel
       of one of the Milky Way's wingtips.

      •

An older ham winks out of visible existence then and there.
Once I've spread my parts out beyond recall
         I won't care.
      The effigy's upkeep will fall to a younger tortoise.
This admittedly better than nothing, but we have plinths to sector,
       images to cleave, dinette sets to splinter, holograms to appease.

      •

I walk to the person and just begin speaking about why I quit painting.
We agree that not only is there no time to get anything done,
                there's in fact no time—it's all a scam
            disguising absolute lack of duration and event, total bullshit.
We sit still as eggs uncracked and children foaming beneath us.
I haven't been in this sort of suburban supermarket in decades.
I'd forgotten the vastness of vegetable enterprise. The difference
between don't know, won't know, can't know, and bad throw
                sails over the cutoff's head and nails a peanut vendor.

·

My reappearance—which I watch from a third-person
            angle bracket affixed high in extradimensional game room—
is met with anxiety by remaining conspirators
            all of whom have faded back into innocuous clerical labor,
perhaps waiting to reemerge, perhaps done with all that now.
            Where'd I been and through what agency so thoroughly
                transformed? How do they know I'm who I
            appear to be, and if I am, on whose or what's
behalf have I now rippled the surface of this denouement?

·

Decades from now giant swine own the landscape
            and jellyfish armies leave the sea to fight them.
An armless, eyeless, earless being, size of a doll,
            translucent as a peeled lychee nut, somehow
fallen into our responsibility, the two of us
            who live as monarchs on a pedestal high above the billions-
teeming territory to which we descend to buy canned mud.
Main characters thus established, we can proceed
            to the tale proper.

EDGE BOOKS

AERIAL MAGAZINE

(EDITED BY ROD SMITH)

Literature published by Aerial/Edge is available through Small Press Distribution (www.spdbooks.org; 1-800-869-7553; orders@spdbooks.org) or from the publisher at P.O. Box 25642, Georgetown Station, Washington, D.C. 20027. When ordering from Aerial/Edge directly, add $2.00 postage for individual titles. Two or more titles postpaid. For more information, please visit our Web site at www.aerialedge.com.